ASANTE

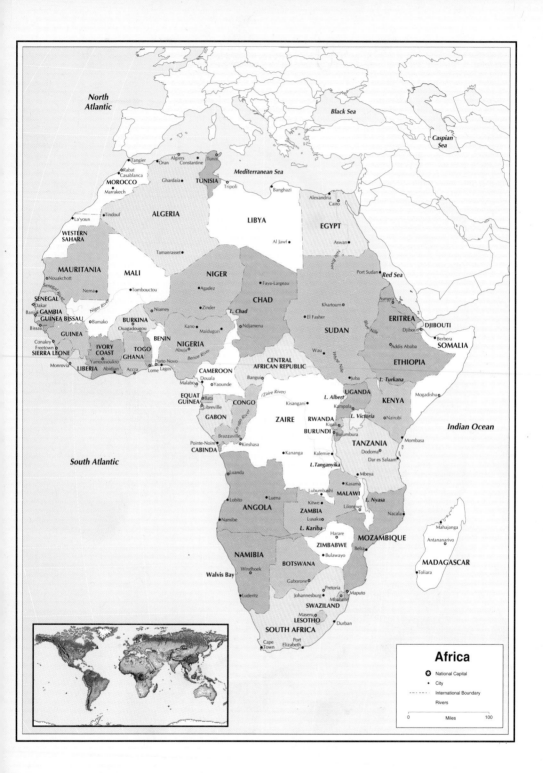

North
Atlantic

Black Sea

Caspian
Sea

Tangier
Oran Algiers Constantine Tunis
Rabat
Casablanca
MOROCCO
Ghardaia
TUNISIA
Tripoli
Mediterranean Sea
Banghazi
Marrakech
Alexandria
Cairo
La'youn
Tindouf
ALGERIA
LIBYA
EGYPT
WESTERN
SAHARA
Al Jawf
Aswan
Tamanrasset
MAURITANIA
MALI
NIGER
Port Sudan
Red Sea
Nouakchott
Agadez
Faya-Largeau
Asmera
Nema
Tombouctou
CHAD
Khartoum
ERITREA
SENEGAL
Niamey
Zinder
Djibouti
DJIBOUTI
Dakar
Bamako
Kano
Ndjamena
El Fasher
SUDAN
Addis Ababa
Berbera
SOMALIA
Banjul GAMBIA
GUINEA BISSAU
BURKINA
Ouagadougou
Maiduguri
Bissau
BENIN
NIGERIA
Wau
White Nile
ETHIOPIA
GUINEA
Conakry
IVORY
COAST
TOGO
Abuja
Benue River
CENTRAL
AFRICAN REPUBLIC
Juba
L. Turkana
Freetown
GHANA
Pinto Novo
Bangui
SIERRA LEONE
Yamoussoukro
Accra Lome Lagos
CAMEROON
UGANDA
KENYA
Mogadishu
Monrovia
LIBERIA
Abidjan
Douala
Yaounde
L. Albert
EQUAT.
GUINEA
Bata
CONGO
Kisangani
Kampala
Malabo
(Zaire River)
L. Victoria
Nairobi
Libreville
ZAIRE
RWANDA
GABON
Kigali
Indian Ocean
South Atlantic
Brazzaville
BURUNDI
Mombasa
Pointe-Noire
Kinshasa
Bulumbura
TANZANIA
CABINDA
Kananga
Kalemie
Dodoma
Dar es Salaam
Luanda
L.Tanganyika
Mbeya
Kasama
Lobito
Luena
Lubumbashi
MALAWI
L. Nyasa
ANGOLA
Kitwe
Lilongwe
Nacala
Namibe
ZAMBIA
Lusaka
L. Kariba
MOZAMBIQUE
Harare
MADAGASCAR
ZIMBABWE
Beira
Mahajanga
NAMIBIA
Bulawayo
Antananarivo
Walvis Bay
Windhoek
BOTSWANA
Toliara
Gaborone
Pretoria
Luderitz
Johannesburg
Maputo
Mbabane
SWAZILAND
Maseru
LESOTHO
Durban
SOUTH AFRICA
Cape
Town
Port
Elizabeth

Africa

✪ National Capital
• City
---- International Boundary
Rivers

0   Miles   100

The Heritage Library of African Peoples

ASANTE

Faustine Ama Boateng, Ph.D.

THE ROSEN PUBLISHING GROUP, INC.
NEW YORK

To the memory of my grandmother, Nana Yaa Ohenewa, a traditional midwife; and to Dr. Kwame Yeboa Daaku, my maternal uncle, Institute of African Studies, University of Ghana, Legon; and Dr. Mercer Cooke, Romance Languages Department, Howard University, Washington, D.C.

ACKNOWLEDGMENTS CHILDRENS ROOM

I would like to thank Dr. Chukwuma Azuonye for inviting me to contribute to this important project and Dr. Herman F. Bostick for his advice on my first draft. To Dr. Mbye B. Cham and family I say *jërejëf* for inspiring me to return to the Akan source when his big daughter was undertaking a research project on Queen Yaa Asantewa. I reserve a special *meda wase papaapa, me nua Ama* to my sister Alice for information and vital materials from home—Ghana.

Published in 1996 by The Rosen Publishing Group, Inc.
29 East 21st Street, New York, NY 10010

Copyright 1996 by The Rosen Publishing Group, Inc.

First Edition

Manufactured in the United States of America

Library of Congress Cataloging-in-Publication Data

Boateng, Faustine Ama.
    Asante / Faustine Ama Boateng. — 1st ed.
      p.   cm. — (The Heritage library of African peoples)
    Summary: Presents a survey of the culture, history, and contemporary life of the Asante people of Ghana.
    ISBN 0-8239-1975-7
    1. Ashanti (African people)—History—Juvenile literature.
2. Ashanti (African people)—Social life and customs—Juvenile literature. [1. Ashanti (African people) 2. Ghana.] I. Title.
II. Series.
DT507.B53   1996
966.7'018—dc20   96-18429
                                             CIP
                                             AC

Contents

INTRODUCTION

THERE IS EVERY REASON FOR US TO KNOW something about Africa and to understand its past and the way of life of its peoples. Africa is a rich continent that has for centuries provided the world with art, culture, labor, wealth, and natural resources. It has vast mineral deposits, fossil fuels, and commercial crops.

But perhaps most important is the fact that fossil evidence indicates that human beings originated in Africa. The earliest traces of human beings and their tools are almost two million years old. Their descendants have migrated throughout the world. To be human is to be of African descent.

The experiences of the peoples who stayed in Africa are as rich and as diverse as of those who established themselves elsewhere. This series of books describes their environment, their modes of subsistence, their relationships, and their customs and beliefs. The books present the variety of languages, histories, cultures, and religions that are to be found on the African continent. They demonstrate the historical linkages between African peoples and the way contemporary Africa has been affected by European colonial rule.

Africa is large, complex, and diverse. It encompasses an area of more than 11,700,000 square miles. The United States, Europe, and India could fit easily into it. The sheer size is an indication of the continent's great variety in geography, terrain, climate, flora, fauna, peoples, languages, and cultures.

Much of contemporary Africa has been shaped by European colonial rule, industrialization, urbanization, and the demands of a world economic system. For more than seventy years, large regions of Africa were ruled by Great Britain, France, Belgium, Portugal, and Spain. African peoples from various ethnic, linguistic, and cultural backgrounds were brought together to form colonial states.

For decades Africans struggled to gain their independence. It was not until after World War II that the colonial territories became independent African states. Today, almost all of Africa is ruled by Africans. Large numbers of Africans live in modern cities. Rural Africa is also being transformed, and yet its people still engage in many of their customs and beliefs.

Contemporary circumstances and natural events have not always been kind to ordinary Africans. Today, however, new popular social movements and technological innovations pose great promise for future development.

George C. Bond, Ph.D., Director
Institute of African Studies
Columbia University, New York

Rich deposits of Ghanaian gold have been essential to Asante society both for trade and ceremonial use. Seen here is a chief's son displaying a sword-bearer's gold-covered regalia, including the horns on the headdress, a chicken figure in his hands, and a state sword.

1
THE PEOPLE

ON GREAT OCCASIONS, ASANTE DRUMS BEAT out this praise song:

Asante Kotoko   Asante, the Porcupine
Wokum apem aa,   If one thousand were killed,
apem beba!   Instantly a thousand would
                 replace them!

This conveys the determination of the Asante. It enabled them to build an empire. With the same determination, they fiercely resisted British rule in their country. After independence, their country was named Ghana; formerly it was the British colony of the Gold Coast.

Ghana was the first European colony in Africa to free itself from European rule. The leading figure in the independence movement was Kwame Nkrumah. He inspired Africans everywhere to fight for their freedom and their rights. He urged Africans and people of African descent to unite in a great Pan-African movement to work for shared goals.

Independent Ghana was named after the great trading Empire of Ghana, which had controlled the region from 700 AD to 1100 AD. Its power and wealth came mainly from gold. Several centuries later, the same became true of the Asante.

For many centuries African gold was traded and exported overland to north Africa and across the Mediterranean by the African empires of Ghana, Mali, and Songhay. This African gold was made into coins by the Arabs. Arabs also supplied Europe with some African gold for a profit. This gold-producing part of Africa was therefore of great world importance. Europeans wanted to trade directly with the gold producers, but the Arabs guarded the secret trade routes across the Sahara Desert.

When European ships developed the technology of movable sails in the 1400s—something the Arabs had used for centuries—they could finally approach the gold-producing regions from the sea. In about 1470 Portuguese ships finally reached the Gold Coast. The Portuguese found abundant supplies of gold in the coastal villages. They built several fortresses there. The largest, called Elmina (the Mine), was visited in 1482 by Christopher Columbus. Soon other

Today, most Asante live in the country of Ghana. Historically, the Asante kingdom was associated with the forest region that now falls into the Asante District. Since the Asante have historically lived in Ghana's interior, some distance from coastal ports, their gold trade with the Europeans had to go through coastal Akan groups, such as the Fante.

European nations began to compete for the gold trade. The Dutch took over Elmina in 1637. Between them, the British, Dutch, Danish, and Swedish established about sixty trading settlements along the coast of Ghana in the 1600s and 1700s. The ancient trade routes across the Sahara Desert were quickly redirected toward the new buyers at the coast.

At first, gold was traded for European goods, including C-shaped ingots of copper and brass (called *manilas*), guns, cloth and clothing, household items, and tools. Experts estimate that between 1400 and 1900 about 15 million ounces of gold were exported from this region. From the 1700s on, however, slaves were more important for trade than gold. European records show that almost 700,000 slaves were taken from the Gold Coast to the Americas in the 1700s. The actual figure would have been much higher, because many slaves were traded unofficially.

The coast and the interior of Ghana and parts of Côte d'Ivoire are home to several Akan peoples. They have similar cultures and languages, but there is a long history of competition and warfare between their small states. Two of the most prominent Akan groups are the Asante, who lived in the forested central region that is rich in gold deposits, and the Fante, who lived along the coast and dominated trade with the Europeans at Elmina.

The Asante people's rise to power was based on three key factors: unity, military strength, and control of trade. By defeating and uniting with

Founded as the capital of the Asante kingdom in the 1690s, Kumase is now the second largest city in Ghana. Seen here is downtown Kumase, the commercial and transportation center of the Asante area of Ghana.

other small Akan states, the Asante were able to overthrow the coastal states, which acted as middlemen in the European gold trade, and deal directly with the traders themselves.

The Asante Empire was founded in the 1690s by Osei Tutu, the first Asantehene (King of the Asante), with the help of his best friend, Okomfo Anokye, the high priest. They established a strong kingdom, with Kumase as its capital. Kumase was named after a shady *kuma* tree that was the sacred center of the city until the British chopped it down. Today Kumase is the second largest city in Ghana. It is still the capital of the Asante region.

It is not known exactly when the Asante

arrived in this area. Before 1500 the five important states of the Twi-speaking Akan peoples were Adanse, Akyem, Assin, Denkyira, and Asante. According to Akan tradition, it was in Adanse that Onyankopon Kwame, the Supreme Being, began the creation of the world. Adanse is thus regarded by the Akan as the origin of the founding fathers of the five major states. Many members of the eight principal Asante clans still consider Adanse to be their ancestral home.

By the 1580s there were several small groups of Akan scattered throughout the forest zone of Ghana. The northwestern section of this region contained rich gold fields and sought-after kola nuts. Trade linked this area to the Mali Empire, the state of Bono-Manso, and other powerful kingdoms in the region. The Akan of the forest zone had the added advantage of living in a fertile region watered by three important rivers: the Pra, the Oda, and the Ofin. Today most of the Akan peoples, including the Asante, still live in this forest region of Ghana.▲

chapter

2

SOCIETY AND RELIGION

▼ THE ASANTE FAMILY ▼

The primary social unit is the extended family, those linked by blood ties. The Asante have eight major clans: Aduana, Agona, Asakyiri, Asenee, Asona, Bretuo, Ekoona, and Oyoko. Each clan is divided into subgroups. A clan is founded on common lineage. Members of the same clan cannot marry because they are believed to be descended from a common female ancestor.

Descent and inheritance are determined by a matrilineal system—that is, through the female ancestors of the mother's side of the family. This means that children are much more closely connected to their mother's family (*abusua*), especially to their uncles, than to their father's family. A son does not inherit his father's wealth and titles, but those of his matrilineal uncle (his mother's brother). Today the clan system seldom has political or economic importance, but it still has significance in religious life.

According to Asante customary law, marriage is the vital force that links two large extended families through the bride. Asante marriage is usually polygynous, meaning the husband can have more than one wife.

Each extended family of the same female line, or *abusua*, worships the same matrilineal ancestors. *Abusua* members perform regular ceremonies to honor the *abusua* ancestors, whose spirits are believed to be always present. Family life and structure therefore have important spiritual aspects.

Each family has a leader or family head known as *abusuapanyin*. He is responsible for the material and spiritual welfare of every member of the *abusua*. A number of subheads are also selected from each household within the large village of *abusua* relatives. The *abusuapanyin* controls the land farmed by the members. He also maintains law, order, justice, and harmony.

▼ THE ASANTE COMMUNITY ▼

Although not all members of Asante villages necessarily share blood ties, the head of the *abusua* lineage and other *abusua* elders lead the community. The elders settle internal disputes among members of the *abusua*.

The main symbol of authority for Asante rulers is the *akondwa*, or stool. Seen here is an Asante man carving a stool, which may later be adorned with beads, shells, or precious stones.

The symbol of authority among the *abusua-panyin* and every Asante ruler is *akondwa*, the stool. A chief is said to occupy or sit on an *akondwa*, but such stools are never actually sat upon. A person who is chosen to be chief is said to be enstooled. When deposed, or removed from office, he or she is said to be destooled. The stool may be carved and blackened, or adorned with precious stones, beads, or cowrie shells.

As the population grows and the community expands, people build more villages nearby. These villages later develop into a town. In the past, each *abusua* dominated a section of a town. While the family is the basic political unit in the village, the town becomes a complex political unit, exercising political authority over a wider area. It also develops social and trading relationships with other *nkuro*, towns, within the *oman*, state.

The enstoolment of an Asante chief is an important occasion, and it is accompanied by both ceremony and festivities. Seen here (top) are the official enstoolment ceremony with the leading figures of the community, and (bottom) some of the festivities surrounding the enstoolment in Kumase.

All Akan land was organized into states. Each *oman* was headed by an Omanhene. A state had several social, religious, and political divisions. For instance, there were chiefs, sub-chiefs, councils of elders, traditional religious leaders or priests, and organized groups of young men and artisans. Precolonial Asante society thus consisted of many political units. The primary objective of these units was to work together to ensure the economic and spiritual well-being of the people. Villages that made up the towns shared resources of land and water with other villages. The sense of sharing and caring for one another was and still is encouraged in young people from an early age. This strengthens the unity and harmony of the group. The system was designed to serve community needs. The emphasis is still placed upon communal life. Thus the *abusua* remains the basic political unit.

In the 1600s all Akan states had traditional rulers and political systems. Despite this fact, only the Asante established a central administration and bureaucracy. This occurred at the court of the great Asantehene Osei Tutu in Kumase, the Asante capital.

▼ TRADITIONAL AND ▼
INFORMAL EDUCATION

Giving a child early instruction in traditional culture is important to Asante society. In this culture, seven- to twelve-year-olds have a great deal of responsibility. They are accountable for their actions, moral obligations, and social duties to the family and the society. Education is an attempt to integrate young people into society and to guide their participation. Together the nuclear and extended families are the primary agents of instruction. The village community is the secondary agent.

Informal education teaches young Asante how to behave, how to preserve marriage, and how to follow customs and traditions. Formal education includes the teaching of particular subjects, trades, and professions. It also tells young people how to lead productive lives in Ghana and the modern world.

In traditional Asante society, particularly in rural Ghana, the man is considered the breadwinner. The boys are generally taught their father's occupation through direct participation. If the father is a cocoa farmer, the sons are also trained to work on the farm. If a son lives with his maternal uncle, the boy almost always follows the uncle's profession. A traditional priest, herbalist, or diviner instructs only his favorite son or nephew in his art.

Mothers or grandmothers teach girls household management through direct participation. A girl who is incapable of carrying out household chores is usually the object of scorn. "Shame on you," a mother is often heard

Traditionally, marriage has played an important role in Asante society. The Christian marriage ceremony seen here displays both contemporary and traditional Asante dress.

scolding a lazy daughter. "I really sympathize with the man who will have the misfortune of taking you for a wife."

▼ MARRIAGE ▼

Marriage is considered very important, so parents are particularly concerned about whom their child marries. It is often said that when a woman marries she does not marry one man but rather a whole family. A marriage that is not approved by the parents of both parties can fall apart under the pressure from one or both families.

When a boy is old enough, his parents take the initiative—sometimes it is still considered their right—to find him a wife. They search for a

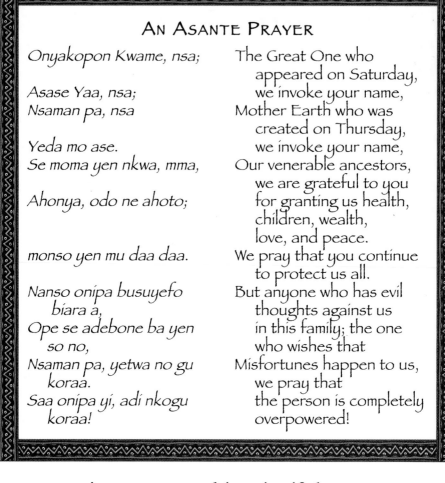

AN ASANTE PRAYER

Onyakopon Kwame, nsa;	The Great One who appeared on Saturday, we invoke your name,
Asase Yaa, nsa;	
Nsaman pa, nsa	Mother Earth who was created on Thursday,
Yeda mo ase.	we invoke your name,
Se moma yen nkwa, mma,	Our venerable ancestors, we are grateful to you
Ahonya, odo ne ahoto;	for granting us health, children, wealth, love, and peace.
monso yen mu daa daa.	We pray that you continue to protect us all.
Nanso onipa busuyefo biara a,	But anyone who has evil thoughts against us
Ope se adebone ba yen so no,	in this family; the one who wishes that
Nsaman pa, yetwa no gu koraa.	Misfortunes happen to us, we pray that
Saa onipa yi, adi nkogu koraa!	the person is completely overpowered!

prospective partner and inquire if there are any dangerous diseases, such as tuberculosis, leprosy, or madness, in her family. Today parents also check for drug abuse and AIDS. The girl's family makes similar inquiries. Sometimes the betrothal occurs at a very young age, and the girl goes to live with her future parents-in-law to be trained in household management. This ensures the wife's loyalty and wards off other suitors.

▼ RELIGIOUS INSTRUCTION ▼

The instruction of young people includes training in ancestral worship. It emphasizes spiritual and moral values and awe of the gods. Every clan has its own religious focus on ancestors and gods.

The priest's role is as a man with supernatural powers who dispels the effects of witchcraft. He never hesitates to tell the parents of a sick child the names of witches in their family. The priest explains how they harbor evil thoughts to destroy the family's reputation or to kill some of their relatives. He asks the parents to make sacrifices to their deities and ancestors, who are eager to protect their grandchildren.

Children are taught that ancestors are the "living-dead," to whom members of the clan convey their prayers. A mother holding her sick child will pray to an ancestor to cure the child. She will also go to see a native herbalist or a priest in hopes of curing the child.

In Asante, and Akan tradition in general, offerings and sacrifices are used to communicate with ancestors and the gods. By paying particular attention to funeral rites, adults set an example of how young people should behave toward the dead. For example, as an elder pours a libation, he thanks the ancestral gods and asks that goodness, health, success, and prosperity will bless the *abusua*.

AKAN SYMBOLS AND PROVERBS

Symbols play an important role in the different Akan societies. These symbols appear in many forms, whether they are stamped on *adinkra* cloth, carved into a wooden chief's stool, or on goldweights. Often, Akan rulers and other important people have objects, carved from wood and covered in gold or silver, attached to their umbrellas, state swords, and other regalia. They come in the forms of humans, animals, plants, and other common objects, but they are not merely used for ornamentation. Rather, these symbolic objects contain rich meaning. They remind viewers of Akan proverbs, wise sayings about different aspects of life.

Symbol: Man holding an egg
Proverb: Power is like an egg—when held firmly, it does not break. But when held loosely, it falls from one's grasp and shatters into pieces.
Meaning: Suggests that it is necessary for one to keep a firm grip on power.

Symbol: Porcupine
Proverb: You can tell from the quills of a porcupine whether it is prepared to fight or not.
Meaning: Suggests the readiness of the Asante nation to wage war on its enemies.
Proverb: One should never rub up against a porcupine.
Meaning: Don't start a fight with someone more powerful than you, for you will almost certainly lose.

Symbol: Man following an elephant
Proverb: Those who follow an elephant do not get wet from the dew.
Meaning: Powerful men protect their followers.

Symbol: Chicken head
Proverb: You don't need a big stick to crack a chicken's skull.
Meaning: Small issues require small responses, while more important ones call for more serious action. Don't make a mountain out a molehill.

Symbol: One man lying face up and another lying face down
Proverb: You complain that you cannot see God while resting on your back; do you think I can see Him lying with my nose to the ground?
Meaning: Suggests that much is expected from those who are more fortunate than others.

Symbol: Leopard
Proverb: Although the rain wets the leopard's spots, it does not wash them off.
Meaning: Whatever happens, a person's true nature never changes.

Symbol: Blooming palm tree
Proverb: While other trees lose their leaves, the palm tree's leaves will always remain fresh.
Meaning: A wish for long life and prosperity.

Symbol: The frame of a shield
Proverb: When a shield wears out, its framework still remains.
Meaning: Although all men die, their good deeds and wisdom will live on after their death.

Symbol: Two birds struggling for a cockroach
Proverb: Birds will not spare a cockroach that comes into their midst.
Meaning: One who falls victim to his enemies can expect little mercy.

Symbol: Wisdom knot
Proverb: The knot that is tied by a wiseman cannot be untied by a fool.
Meaning: The leader has a right to his position by virtue of his superior wisdom.

Symbol: A flock of birds on a tree
Proverb: Only birds of the same species will interact on a tree.
Meaning: Birds of a feather flock together; it stresses the importance of one's lineage.

Because ancestors are so highly respected in Asante religious traditions, funerals are extremely important events. Above, black-clad Asante gather for a funeral ceremony.

At funeral ceremonies young girls learn by listening to the women singing dirges—a solemn kind of poetry—to honor a dead relative.

Informal education also involves listening to myths, legends, folktales, proverbs, riddles, songs, and rhymes. These oral accounts convey moral messages, wisdom, philosophy, and the Asante outlook on life.

Traditional informal education in Asante society thus reinforces and continues the cultural system—language, social values, laws, and customs—that is essential for the survival of the community. Today many Asante elders resist change and Western influence, because they believe that their traditional system equips young people with all the knowledge, skills, and beliefs that they will need to become responsible adults. ▲

chapter

3

ART

IN THE PAST, ASANTE ARTISTS AND craftspeople made prestigious items solely for the Asantehene, the royal family, and distinguished members of the court. They specialized in goldwork, woven *kente* cloth, wooden sculpture, metalwork, beadwork, and pottery.

▼ GOLDWEIGHTS ▼

Asante goldsmiths are famous for making goldweights that are used to weight the scales that measured the value of gold being traded. Every Akan gold trader needed a set of goldweights to weigh out gold dust and nuggets. Each goldweight is a beautiful miniature sculpture of copper, bronze, or brass. They depict humans, animals, insects, and objects of daily life. Most also illustrate a character or event in the history or proverbs of the Asante. A weight in the shape of a crocodile, for example, is a reminder of this proverb: "When you are safe on the river bank, then you can tell the crocodile by the lump on its snout." The proverb warns against upsetting dangerous people unless you are safely beyond their reach. Apart from its beauty and meaning, every weight had to function as an accurate counterweight.

Today priceless goldweights are kept safely as "stool property" in the Asante royal treasury. Some wealthy elders have hidden their goldweights as part of the treasure of the clan. Such weights and contemporary reproductions are now popular with collectors worldwide.

In every family there are grandmothers, custodians of tradition, who keep their trousseau of gold jewelry. On ceremonial occasions,

Asante goldweights once had practical use for weighing gold dust or nuggets and are now highly valued art. This goldweight of a rider shows great attention to detail.

such as birth, marriage, and festivals, the Asante wear their gold jewelry and gorgeous *kente* cloths.

▼ WEAVING ▼

Asante weavers continue to make creative designs that reflect their history, culture, and many other aspects of their society. Asante *kente* cloth is made from many handwoven strips that are about four inches wide. The strips are sewn together to form large pieces of cloth. *Kente* cloths come in various rich colors, sizes, and beautiful designs. Each color and design has a symbolic meaning.

Oral tradition states that Asante *kente* weaving was invented in the 1600s by Ota Kraban and Kwaku Ameyaw, who lived in Bonwire, which is now the center of the *kente* industry. They observed a spider weaving its web, and concluded that it was similar to the art of weaving mats from *kenten* plant fibre. They developed the skill of *kente* weaving, which soon came to the attention of the Asantehene of that time. He admired the *kente* and made a law that *kente* was royal cloth. The weavers used silk threads to make *kente* exclusively for the Asantehene and the royal family, inventing special designs to gain their favor. The weavers became more and more creative as they tried to outdo one another. Prestigious *kente* cloth was worn on special

Weaving detailed, meaningful patterns of *kente* cloth is highly skilled work. Above, an Asante weaver creates *kente* cloth on a loom.

KENTE

High-quality *kente* cloth is woven in rich, symbolic colors of gold (symbolizing gold dust and nuggets); yellow (the yolk of the egg); blue (the sky and abode of the Supreme Being); red (sacrificial blood); green (forests and agriculture); maroon (Mother Earth, the symbol of fertility and protection against evil spirits); pink and purple (associated with feminine aspects of life—tenderness, kindness, and love); and black (the color of the ancestors and spirituality).

NAMES OF *KENTE* CLOTHS

All the names of *kente* designs are in Twi.

- **Adwinasa** means "all motifs were used up." This name indicates that the weaver included numerous motifs to outdo his rivals and please the king. *Adwinasa* was exclusively worn by the Asante kings and later by wealthy and distinguished people. The design symbolizes royalty, wealth, elegance, and superior creativity.
- **Obaakofo mmu man** means "one person cannot rule a nation." This design evokes the traditional Akan principle of democratic cooperation.
- **Sika Futuro** means "gold dust," which was the currency before coins and paper bills were introduced. The cloth symbolizes wealth, prosperity, and enterprise.
- **Frempoma** was the name of the queen mother of Bonwire—the center of *kente* weavers—and of some important Akan queens. This *kente* cloth reflects motherhood, maturity, love, and harmony.
- **Wofro Dua Pa a Na Yepia Wo** means "one who climbs a good fruit tree, people will push him to share the fruits. They will certainly enjoy his labor." It represents hope, sharing, mutual respect and benefits, and caring.
- **Nkontompo Ntoman** means the cloth of a liar. It expresses dislike of dishonesty, deceitful acts, and lies.

Once a royal cloth woven only for the Asantehene, *kente* is now popular throughout the world. Seen here is an Asante chief in ceremonial regalia, wearing *kente* cloth.

occasions, such as when the Asantehene paraded through the streets. Today *kente* continues to be worn at such events.

In the 1950s *kente* cloth was still very expensive and worn only on special occasions. In 1957 Ghana's first president, Osagyefo Kwame Nkrumah, and members of Parliament wore good-quality *kente* cloth frequently. Today *kente* is very popular in many West African countries and overseas, particularly in the United States. It is now commercially produced, and often *kente* designs are printed onto other fabric. However, the best-quality *kente* is still hand-woven, and its traditional designs refer to oral tradition, history, and religious, moral, and social values.

The Asante also wear *adinkra* cloth. This kind of cloth is decorated with designs that are stamped onto cloth. Like goldweights, these designs often have special meanings. *Adinkra* cloth was once worn mainly at funerals. People wore different color cloths, depending on their relationship to the deceased. Today there are many new symbols stamped on *adinkra* cloth, and people wear *adinkra* on occasions other than funerals.

▼ OTHER ARTS ▼

The specialized Asante artisans were well organized. Blacksmiths were in charge of state

Once made exclusively for the Asante royalty and spiritual leaders, *adinkra* cloth is now made for other uses, including festival clothing, interior decorations, and book covers. Here, a young man prepares to stamp a pattern on an *adinkra* cloth.

swords, shields, and traditional weapons. Other craftsmen made *ahenemma*, the royal sandals, and various items of regalia in gold, silver, and ivory. In present-day Ghana, the Asantehene, his chiefs, sub-chiefs, and elders still use many traditional items: *kente*, *adinkra*, gold jewelry, state swords, head-dresses, umbrellas, palan-quins, and drums. The soul-washer's disc is worn by officials who purify the ruler's soul at special annual festivals. The ruler's spokesman, or linguist, carries a wooden staff that is covered in gold. The tops of these staffs are beautifully carved with traditional and symbolic designs, like the goldweights.

Asante women who hope to become pregnant carry an *akuaba* doll (discussed on page 37). The woman treats the doll like a real infant once it has been blessed by a priest. *Akuaba* figures, like the one above, illustrate Asante concepts of beauty, such as a high forehead and a small mouth.

MUSIC AND CEREMONY

Almost every Asante ceremony involves music for singing and dancing.

At an Asante religious ceremony, several musical instruments may be played. Gongs, bells, and sometimes xylophones create different pitches of vibrating sounds. The rhythm of drums, made of hollowed gourds or wood, almost always accompanies the dancing and singing of a festival. The beats, pauses, and pitches of the drums also convey specific messages. Like a complex language, the drumbeats may tell of a particular event, such as a coming war or the entrance of the Asantehene. It is from these expressive rhythms that the drums get their name "talking drums."

Wind instruments, such as talking horns, create beautiful melodies that accompany the drummer's beat or are sometimes played alone. Like the talking drums, the notes of horns can also convey messages. Each chief has a horn blower who sounds out a particular note. This both identifies the chief and announces his arrival at a state ceremony.

When different instruments are played together in an Asante ceremony, the sounds are both beautiful and meaningful for the participants and observers.

Musical instruments play a key role in Asante ceremonies. Seen here are a group of talking drummers.

In Asante ceremonies, the notes played on horns often convey particular messages. Seen here, a group of Asante musicians play their talking horns.

Carvers also made other wooden sculptures, such as dolls, called *akuaba*. Women who hoped to become pregnant carried a doll on their back. Today dolls are mostly carved to sell to tourists and art collectors.

▼ MUSIC ▼

Even before Osei Tutu, the first Asantehene, was enstooled, Asante history and proverbs were passed on through horns, flutes, and drums. These were played by the traditional musicians of the Ohene (the chief). Today, at important Asante festivals, the talking drums, accompanied by song, convey messages of historical, social, and political events. Akan languages are tonal, meaning that a word has different meanings, depending on whether it is said with a high, middle, or low tone. Musical instruments can imitate these tones, so that the instruments seem to speak.▲

37

chapter

4
HISTORY

▼ THE FIRST ASANTEHENE ▼

In the mid-1600s Obiri Yeboa of the Oyoko clan led the Asante. He was the maternal grand-uncle of Osei Tutu, who was his heir according to matrilinear inheritance rules.

Osei Tutu's birth was a gift from the gods. His mother, Manu Kotosii, had been married for many years but remained childless. In traditional Asante society a stigma is attached to a barren woman—one who cannot have children. It was thus a great tragedy for a ruler's sister, daughter, or niece to be childless. Manu Kotosii was sent for traditional fertility treatment so that she could bear sons of royal blood. These sons would succeed their powerful maternal uncle, Obiri Yeboa. Manu Kotosii traveled with some relatives from Asante to Akwapem, where they consulted the most powerful deities of the area. Fortunately, she responded very well to the herbal treatment and the prayers to the Otutu gods of that area. Manu had a son. To thank and honor the Otutu gods, she called him Osei Tutu.

Osei Tutu grew up to be an intelligent, honest, and brave young man. His great-uncle, Obiri Yeboa, sent him to learn diplomacy and customary laws at the court of Boa Amponsem, the ruler of Denkyira. By the 1660s Denkyira was a powerful overlord state. It controlled the forest zone's trade in gold, kola nuts, and slaves who were captured in wars.

The Agona clan of the Adanse region had defeated other small states and set up the powerful state of Denkyira. They had access to the coast where Europeans, such as the Portuguese, the Dutch, and the British, had long built forts and castles as trading posts. Akan groups on the coast, such as the Fante and the people of Denkyira, traded gold and slaves for firearms and other goods from the Europeans. They used the firearms to wage wars against their weaker neighbors and enslave them. Weaker states, as Asante was then, had to pay tribute to Denkyira. Asante and similar states in the interior had no access to the coastal trade, so they could not profit directly by selling the things they produced—like gold. They had to deal through the states that controlled the coast.

While Osei Tutu was living in Denkyira, he fell in love with Bensua, the sister of Boa

Amponsem, the Denkyirahene (meaning King of Denkyira). Afraid for his life, Osei Tutu escaped from Denkyira to the state of Akwamu. Akwamu is where the deities of Otutu had blessed his mother Manu Kotosii, where Osei Tutu was born, and where he had the protection and friendship of the ruler. Around 1689 Osei Tutu's great-uncle, Obiri Yeboa, was killed in an ambush near the River Pra. His sudden death changed the life of young Osei Tutu. An important dele-gation from Asante immedi-ately traveled to announce the news to Osei Tutu and bring him back to Asante.

Asante hunters traditionally cover their clothes with talismans, which protect the hunter from his prey and give him luck on the hunt. Here, an Asante hunter at a public ceremony wears traditional cloth- and leather-covered talismans while carrying a modern rifle.

Diplomatic and kind, the ruler of Akwamu selected an escort of soldiers to protect young Osei Tutu and his delegation on their way to Asante, where Osei Tutu was enstooled as Asantehene, King of the Asante.

During the years Osei Tutu spent in the states of Akwamu and Denkyira, he won the favor and friendship of important men at court. It was probably in Denkyira that he met his best friend, Okomfo Anokye, a celebrated high priest who joined the young king soon after his enstoolment.

Traditionally, Asante chiefs have linguists, or spokesmen, who speak for them during ceremonies and meetings. Seen here is a linguist carrying the staff, which is his symbol of office. It is carved from wood, and the top is covered with gold foil.

Okomfo Anokye provided Osei Tutu with good political advice and spiritual strength.

▼ THE REIGN OF OSEI TUTU ▼

At the beginning of his reign, Osei Tutu faced numerous problems. Several small Akan states remained independent despite their similar culture and religions. Some of the clans conquered by Obiri Yeboa rejected the young Osei Tutu's rule. For example, Osafo Akoto, the ruler of Tafo state, considered Osei Tutu too young and inexperienced, so he defied him. The most difficult problem that Osei Tutu faced was his own people. They were restless and discontented. They wanted to avenge the death of Obiri Yeboa, and they were also tired of paying tribute to Denkyira.

Determined to build a strong political force against Denkyira, Osei Tutu planned to unite the small Akan states and build a powerful army to defeat Denkyira and gain access to the coast. Upon reaching the coast, the Asante army would conquer the coastal peoples who controlled trade with the Europeans. To do so he would have to defeat many neighboring states around Asante and those in the south and west of present-day Ghana, most of which had purchased firearms from the Europeans. When he conquered them, he would confiscate their weapons, train them in the Asante army, and crush any resistant state.

Osei Tutu used both diplomacy and force. He married a young woman from the royal Aduana clan before he defeated their state, Kaase. Soon after, he made the Kaasehene the overlord of his household and gave him the title Gyaasehene, meaning chief of the Asantehene's bodyguards, a division of the Asante army. Next, Osei Tutu conquered the important state of Amakom and its ruler, Akosa Yiadom. Later, Osei Tutu arranged for his niece to marry the next Amakomhene. This arranged royal marriage was another skillful diplomatic move, because her son would be enstooled as the next Asantehene according to the matrilineal custom. These two defeated rulers became strong supporters of Osei Tutu.

Osei Tutu had to use force to incorporate states in the southwest of Ghana. He defeated the state of Tafo, captured its ruler, Osafo Akoto, and brought home treasure that included a gold guitar. He incorporated Tafo into the growing Asante state and gave Osafo Akoto the title Benkumhene, commander in chief of the left wing of the army.

Strengthened by these victories, Osei Tutu turned against more powerful enemies such as the fierce Domaa at Suntreso near Kumase. The Domaa were defeated and fled to the west of the forest area, where they founded the state of Gyaman.

In spite of all his victories, Osei Tutu still continued to pay tribute to the Denkyirahene. Furthermore, all the states he controlled— Asumenya, Dwaben, Kokofu, Nsuta, and Mampon—remained subjects of the Denkyirahene. Their fervent desire was to become independent because, like Osei Tutu, they belonged to the Oyoko clan. Osei Tutu united the clan to defeat Denkyira and free the Asante state.

▼ OSEI TUTU AND OKOMFO ANOKYE: ▼ LOYAL FRIENDS

Okomfo Anokye, the famous high priest, was named Kwame Agyei Frempon at birth. His title Okomfo (priest) Anokye emphasizes his accomplishments and miraculous deeds for Asanteman, the state of Asante. According to Denkyira traditions, his mother was a native of this state, and he trained to be a priest there. However, traditions in Akwapem state claim that he was born and raised at Akwugua, where people now point out his home to tourists. Okomfo Anokye could belong to both places, since Denkyira and Akwapem are matrilineal and patrilineal respectively, and his father may have been from Akwapem.

Okomfo Anokye and Osei Tutu may have first met at the court of the Denkyirahene, but their friendship developed later in Akwamu state.

ASANTE SHRINE HOUSES

Certain Akan peoples, including the Asante, often build special shrine houses to pay homage to some of their deities. Akan priests also go here to make sacrifices, to conduct prayers, and to perform other religious ceremonies.

Like symbolic objects and *adinkra* cloths, the sculpted images on the outside walls of the shrine houses are meant to remind observers of Akan proverbs and religious messages. Near the top of this Asante shrine house, facing the door, is the image of a large crocodile biting a small animal. Below that stand two clay human figures—one male, one female. Also, s-shaped forms wind their way about the left side of the building.

Historically, shrine houses were built with high, thatched roofs. But more recently, they are often topped with metal roofs, like the Asante shrine house below.

An Asante shrine house.

After Osei Tutu's enstoolment, Okomfo Anokye became his primary adviser. During this historical period, there was a very close relationship between Akan rulers and priests.

Each Akan state was considered sacred because it was inhabited by spirits of the ancestors and deities. A ruler's political duties were thus linked to spiritual and moral aspects of life. The high priest helped the ruler to observe regular prayers. He also performed numerous religious ceremonies for the divine protection and security of the king and the nation. A state priest like Okomfo Anokye did for the state what the *abusua* head does for his lineage. In both cases the ever-present ancestors, who own the land and its people, had to be frequently attended to. This was an essential duty when the welfare of the entire state was at stake. A ruler or any other authority who failed to consult a priest would be doomed. Many held Okomfo Anokye in awe.

Today he is still regarded as an illustrious high priest by the Asante and many other Akan. Okomfo Anokye's greatest "miracle" was the creation of the Golden Stool—the soul of the Asante.

▼ THE GOLDEN STOOL—THE SOUL ▼
OF THE ASANTE

Osei Tutu and Asanteman, the state of

The famous Golden Stool is only brought out for very special occasions. Seen here is the 1985 fiftieth anniversary celebration of the restoration of the Asante throne. The present Asantehene, Opoku Ware II, is seated left of center; the Golden Stool is on the right, placed on its own throne, which prevents it from touching the ground.

Asante, lived under the constant threat of the Denkyira. For example, around 1698 the new Denkyirahene, called Ntim Gyakari, humiliated the Asante. According to oral history, he sent a huge brass basin and threatening soldiers to the Asantehene. All Asante chiefs were ordered to fill the basin with gold dust. Each chief was also told to send his youngest wife to the Denkyirahene. Furious and humiliated, Osei Tutu refused to obey.

Conscious of the menace of Denkyira and

foreigners on the coast of Ghana, Okomfo Anokye decided to unite all the small independent Asante states under one king. He assured his best friend Osei Tutu that he would have a powerful army that would win many victories. To fulfill his promise, Okomfo Anokye advised Osei Tutu to summon all Asante chiefs and their people to Kumase, the new capital.

On one Friday, Osei Tutu and all the Asante assembled. At the center of this huge gathering stood the high priest, Okomfo Anokye. He invoked the spirits of the ancestors and the deities. Suddenly, the sky became extremely dark. Amid thunder and lightning, Okomfo Anokye performed a miracle—a glittering stool covered in gold descended from the dark clouds and slowly came to rest on the lap of Osei Tutu. After a thanksgiving prayer, Okomfo Anokye asked all the chiefs to provide nail clippings that he burned and mixed with medicine. This he used to consecrate the Golden Stool.

Okomfo Anokye named the stool Sika Dwa Kofi, which means Golden Stool Born on Friday. He dedicated this sacred gift to Osei Tutu, to every future Asantehene, to all Asante chiefs, and to Asanteman, the state itself. He declared the Golden Stool the Soul of the Asante Empire, a symbol of unity, victory, and love. He granted its custody to his friend Osei Tutu and all his successors. Okomfo Anokye also

Originally constructed by Portuguese colonists in 1482, Elmina Fortress was occupied and altered by different European powers over the next 400 years. Today the well-preserved fortification is a historic site and museum.

blessed Kumase as the new capital that would be home to all Asante kings and queens.

King Osei Tutu founded Kumase for its strategic position. The city is surrounded by hills and marshy land, making it easy to defend. At Bantama, a suburb of Kumase where the memorable ceremony of the Golden Stool took place, Okomfo Anokye's sword is still stuck in the ground. On that awesome occasion he announced to the gathering that a new era for the Asante had dawned. He buried all the traditional wooden stools of the chiefs and told them to defend only the one national stool—the golden one.

The Golden Stool was a great source of inspiration and unity for the Asante nation. It symbolized the new unity achieved by Osei Tutu's efforts. So long as the Asante stood

Many Asante traditions date back to the years before European colonialism. Seen here is a soul washer's disc, worn by servants of the king. The servants used the disc to cleanse the soul of the ruler.

together, they could defeat their enemies and control the gold trade. This they did for almost 200 years.

▼ AFTER OSEI TUTU ▼

Osei Tutu died around 1712. During the rest of the 1700s, the Asante dominated much of the Gold Coast and Ivory Coast, as they were then known by Europeans. The Portuguese fortress at

Elmina had been taken over by the Dutch in 1637. They traded with the state of Denkyira, which owned the fortress. After Osei Tutu's defeat of Denkyira, the Asante took control of Elmina and the profitable trade with the Dutch. The English traded mainly at Cape Coast with the Fante. The Fante refused to acknowledge Asante authority until they were defeated in 1805. Equally important to the Asante was trade with African states to the north.

The 1800s saw many changes. In the first decades, Kumase was a wealthy, impressive, and important trading center with a population of about 40,000 people. It was visited by Europeans and Arabs, who wrote favorable accounts of the cleanliness and beauty of the capital. The government and civil service managed the large state with great efficiency.

Muslims and Europeans were employed by the state in the second half of the 1800s. Their literacy and other skills assisted the government and helped modernize certain aspects of it.

This strong, successful, and quite international state did have some problems, however. Like many large, centralized empires, it suffered from breakaway groups that challenged its authority and weakened it when they left. Such internal problems enabled the British to take control of the Asante Empire during the colonial period.▲

chapter

5

COLONIZATION

BETWEEN 1884 AND 1894 THE ASANTE Empire experienced a serious political crisis. Fierce disputes within royal families almost destroyed Asante unity. Civil war broke out among the Asante states. The British seized this opportunity. They quickly rushed in to impose their power on the Asante Empire. In 1894, after ten years of civil war, King Prempeh I was enstooled as head of the weakened state. The British sent their government official to live in Kumase. However, King Prempeh I rejected any foreign representative on Asante soil. Therefore, the British launched a massive invasion in 1896. They conquered the Asante Empire and declared it a protectorate. Still there was no peace in the kingdom of Asante.

King Prempeh I boldly refused Britain's demand that he pay the costs of the British invasion. The British arrested and deported him to

the Seychelles Islands, in the Indian Ocean.
Many royals, including his mother and father,
and many important Asante chiefs, were exiled
with the king.

In Akan tradition, royal women have always
played important roles at the courts. Ohemaa,
the queen mother, is often consulted before a
new king or chief is chosen. She can rule when
a chief or king is destooled or dies suddenly.
At this time of crisis, Queen Yaa Asantewa,
queen mother of Edweso, an Asante state about
ten miles east of Kumase, exhibited heroic
leadership.

The British built a fort at Kumase to impose
their authority and presence. From March 25 to
March 28, 1900, Sir Frederick Hodgson, the
governor of the Gold Coast, visited Kumase
with other important British officials. At a public
ceremony, the governor insulted the tradition
and sovereignty of the Asante by ordering Queen
Yaa Asantewa and her people to bring him the
Golden Stool. He wanted to sit on the Golden
Stool, the Soul of Asante. He thought it was a
throne and by sitting on it he would demonstrate that he controlled the Asante. If he had
taken the trouble to know his opponents, he
would have realized that nobody, not even the
Asantehene, ever sat on the Golden Stool. It is a
sacred stool from the ancestral gods.

The disrespect of the British governor was the

final straw for the outraged Queen Yaa
Asantewa. That night the queen mother called
an emergency assembly. She mobilized her
soldiers and ordered them to attack all the
British in Kumase if they did not promise to
return King Prempeh I and the other exiles,
including Queen Yaa Asantewa's own son. At the
same time, Hodgson also sent men to search for
the Golden Stool. Their search was futile; the
sacred stool was securely hidden.

Soon war broke out. Queen Yaa Asantewa and
some of her soldiers were stationed in a dense
forest at Ahafo. The general of the Asante army,
Kofi Kufie, led his troops to fight the British,
who were using modern machine guns. It was a
fierce battle. Dauntless, Queen Yaa Asantewa
encouraged the Asante army to fight to the end.
Stationed at Ahafo forest, she and her army
retreated but never surrendered. Ultimately, the
British needed about 2,000 troops to capture
the Queen and her soldiers. She was exiled to
the Seychelles to join King Prempeh I and her
son, Nana Afrane Kuma.▲

chapter

6

GHANA TODAY

GHANA IS A MODERN AND RAPIDLY
changing society, but to preserve the Asante
heritage is a challenge to all Akan people and to
present-day Ghana. Today ancestral beliefs and
rituals are still observed. Alongside formal education, the Asante continue to impart informal
and traditional instruction to their adolescent
sons and daughters.

Many Ghanaians are Christians. Churches
such as the Presbyterians, Methodists,
Anglicans, and Roman Catholics have been in
Ghana since the last century. They built up
schools, colleges, and hospitals. In many cases,
Ghanaian Christians harmonize Christianity
with aspects of their ancestral beliefs.

Recent years have seen an upsurge of new
evangelical and charismatic churches in Ghana
and other African countries. These new groups
emphasize that a Bible-centered life will bring

55

salvation, blessings, and miracles. Some groups promise blessings in the form of great wealth. These approaches to religion that focus on wealth, lively and joyful church services, and stirring crusades have drawn many new followers, particularly among young people. Many of these groups are far less tolerant of traditional Ghanaian beliefs and customs than the older, more established churches are. It remains to be seen what the future effect of these religious views will be on Ghanaian traditions.

It is clear that many aspects of Ghanaian art and culture that are rooted in Ghanaian beliefs have now become popular throughout the world. The goldsmiths of Kurofofrom, *kente* weavers of Bonwire, and wood sculptors of Sewua village continue to create—so much so that their products are now enjoyed globally. Imitation *kente* is even mass-produced. Americans of African descent and those in the diaspora use various items made of cheaper *kente* cloth. The mace of Clark Atlanta University is based on the staff of a Ghanaian chief. It is designed to symbolize the ideals enshrined in the university's motto: "I'll find a way or make one."

The national government of Ghana has also found many ways to preserve aspects of Asante customs and traditions. The National Cultural Center, the University of Science and Technology in Kumase, the Institute of African

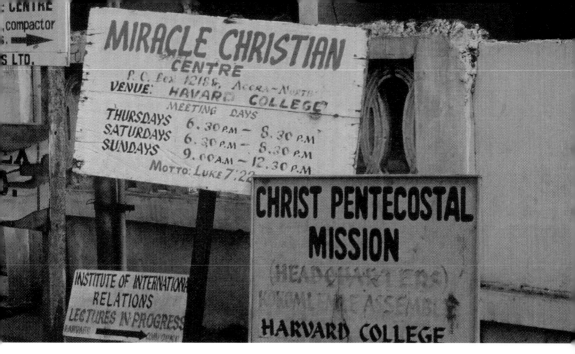

In recent years, there has been an upsurge of Christianity in Ghana. Seen here are a number of Christian signboards in the city of Accra (top), and a signboard advertising the new Action Chapel International in Accra (bottom).

KWAME NKRUMAH (1909–1972)

Nkrumah, the son of a goldsmith, was born in the Gold Coast and trained as a teacher. He continued his studies in the United States at the University of Pennsylvania and at Lincoln University, where the yearbook described him as follows:

Africa is the beloved of his dreams;
Philosopher, thinker, with forceful schemes.

When he sailed out of New York harbor to begin studies at the London School of Economics, he was inspired by the Statue of Liberty, who seemed to be raising her arm to wave goodbye. He said his own farewell to her: "You have opened my eyes to the true meaning of liberty. . . . I shall never rest until I have carried your message to Africa."

Nkrumah lived up to this promise. In London, Nkrumah was asked by an Asante politician to take a leading position in a political party devoted to fighting for the Gold Coast's independence. Over the next few years, Nkrumah led the battle for freedom. He formed his own party. Like his friend the Rev. Martin Luther King, Nkrumah was devoted to non-violent resistance and suffered imprisonment several times.

When the British finally allowed Africans to have representatives in government, Nkrumah, still inside prison, won almost every available vote. He was freed to head an administration that led the Gold Coast to become the first free and independent African country among all the European colonies in Africa. Independent Ghana came into being on March 6, 1957. In 1964 Nkrumah declared Ghana a one-party state and himself life-president. His popularity declined and he was overthrown in 1966. He lived out his exile and continued his writing in Guinea, where President Sékou Touré declared him joint head of state.

Nkrumah's leadership and writings inspired Africans and people of African descent all over the world to fight for their freedom, take pride in their rich heritage, and unite in their common goals. Nkrumah dreamed of a great Pan-African movement that would unite Africans. Today the Organization of African Unity attempts to realize this great ambition.

While Asante traditions continue to be observed throughout Ghana, different aspects of Asante culture are changing along with their country. Seen here, a group of Asante, wearing traditional clothing, prepare to enter a limousine.

Studies at Legon, the National Arts Center, the Ghana News Agency, and Radio Ghana all play a role in achieving this. Radio Ghana starts its early morning transmission by playing the drum music:

Oman Ghana muntie, Ghanafo muntie. . . .

Nation of Ghana, please lend me your ears. . . .

The talking drums salute the entire country and its people in a traditional way before broadcasting the world's news of the day.

Today, the Asante, like other Ghanaians, are involved in a wide variety of jobs. Seen here is a hospital in Ghana.

Today every Ghanaian is very proud of the Asante and Akan traditions as well as those of other ethnic groups in the country. Most of us Ghanaians believe that we must keep traditions that do not slow progress. And we must continue to preserve them in harmony with the broader world of today.▲

Glossary

abusua Mother's family; female lineage.

abusuapanyin Family leader or family head.

adinkra Asante cloth decorated with designs that are stamped on.

ahenemma Royal sandals.

akondwa Stool.

akuaba Wooden dolls that were once carried by Asante women who hoped to become pregnant.

Asantehene King of the Asante.

Asanteman The State of the Asante.

Elmina The Mine—Portugese fortress in Ghana.

goldweight Small sculpture made of copper, bronze, or brass that is used to weigh gold dust and nuggets.

kente Handwoven Asante cloth whose designs and colors bear particular meanings.

matrilineal Tracing descent and inheritance through the female ancestors of the mother's side of the family.

nkuro Town.

oman State.

Sika Dwa Kofi Golden Stool Born on Friday—considered the Soul of the Asante Empire.

For Further Reading

Adzinyah, Abraham et al. *Let Your Voice Be Heard:
Songs from Ghana and Zimbabwe.* Danbury,
CT: World Music Press, 1986.

Anquandah, James. *Rediscovering Ghana's Past.*
White Plains, NY: Longman, 1982.

Catchpole, Brian, and Akinjogdin, I.A. *History of
West Africa in Maps and Diagrams.* White
Plains, NY: Collins Educational, 1983.

Hintz, Martin. *Ghana.* Chicago: Children's
Press, 1987.

Kellner, Doug. *Kwame Nkrumah.* New York:
Chelsea House, 1987.

Ofori-Ansah, Kwaku. *Symbols of Adinkra Cloth.*
Hyattsville, MD: Sankofa, 1978.

FILMS

Arts of Ghana. UCLA Museum of Cultural
History, 1977.

Index

ABOUT THE AUTHOR

Faustine Ama Boateng was born in Ghana. She earned her B.A. in French language and literature from the Université de Besançon, France, and her Ph.D. in African and Caribbean literature from Howard University. Her publications include *La Famille Tano,* published by Macmillan, and *Le Village de Papa,* published by Afram Publications in Ghana. Her articles have appeared in the *Revue Présence Africaine.* She also presented a paper entitled "Adolescence in the Novels of Four Senegalese Women Writers" at an international African conference. Dr. Boateng has taught at Catholic University and Howard University in Washington, DC. She is currently an Assistant Professor of French at Clark Atlanta University in Atlanta, Georgia.

ACKNOWLEDGMENT

The publisher would like to thank Rosalind Hackett, Ph.D., who contributed the section on Christianity in modern Ghana on pages 55 and 56, and the two photographs on page 57.

COMMISSIONING EDITOR
Chukwuma Azuonye, Ph.D.

CONSULTING EDITOR
Gary N. van Wyk, Ph.D.

PHOTO CREDITS
Cover, pp. 8, 30, 32, 34, 40, 41, 45 © Herbert M. Cole; pp. 13, 17, 18 top, 18 bottom, 21, 26, 36, 37, 49, 59, 60 © J. J. Foxx/NYC; pp. 28, 50 © Art Resource; p. 35 © Aldo Tutino/Art Resource; p. 47 © René and Denise David, Switzerland; p. 57 top, 57 bottom © Rosalind Hackett.

LAYOUT AND DESIGN
Kim Sonsky